Original title:
Aloe There, Sunshine

Copyright © 2025 Creative Arts Management OÜ
All rights reserved.

Author: Fiona Harrington
ISBN HARDBACK: 978-1-80581-837-3
ISBN PAPERBACK: 978-1-80581-364-4
ISBN EBOOK: 978-1-80581-837-3

Life's Renewal in the Garden's Light

In the garden where laughter grows,
Plants sing songs that nobody knows.
A worm wiggles, wearing a hat,
While the tomato's having a chat.

Bees in bow ties buzz with flair,
Rabbits hop, without a care.
Carrots dance, the radishes wink,
As flowers spread gossip and ink.

The sun peeks in, grinning wide,
While cucumbers try to hide.
Mice in tuxedos bring the cheese,
As daisies sway in the breeze.

With every sprout, a chuckle near,
In this garden, joy is clear.
So plant a smile, let laughter bloom,
And make your heart a sunny room.

Blossoms Beckoning the Dawn

Morning blooms with silly cheer,
Petals laughing, bright and clear.
Sunshine tickles every leaf,
Nature's giggles, oh what a relief!

Waking up the sleepy bees,
Chasing bugs and playful breeze.
Dew drops sparkling, all aglow,
Dancing flowers steal the show!

Colors of Joy in the Light

Crayons spilled upon the grass,
Each hue winks as critters pass.
Sunbeams shoot like silly darts,
Brightening laughing, joyful hearts.

Chirpy birds in outfits bold,
Strut their stuff, or so I'm told.
Laughter echoes from above,
Nature's choir sings of love!

Embracing the Glow of Life

Balloons float upon the breeze,
Whisking worries with such ease.
Glowworms giggle in the dark,
Lighting paths for the park's lark.

Budding dreams and wishful sighs,
Ticklish moments in disguise.
Life's a party, come and play,
Join the fun, don't just delay!

Nature's Embrace in Radiant Light

Silly shadows play their game,
Jumping high, they're never tame.
Sunshine's brush, a merry sight,
Painting joy with pure delight.

Leaves whisper secrets in the wind,
Comedic tales that won't rescind.
Nature chuckles, full of glee,
Join the fun, now dance with me!

Glorious Days of Leafy Dreams

In the garden, plants do dance,
Waving leaves, they seek their chance.
Oh what fun, a leafy show,
Join the flora, steal the glow.

Sunbeams tickle, laughter's near,
Petals chuckle, nothing to fear.
With every branch, a silly tale,
Whispers fly on a breezy gale.

Nature's Anthem in Radiant Air

Birds are singing silly tunes,
While butterflies chase round the moons.
A breeze arrives, it gives a wink,
Tickles my nose, makes me blink.

The daisies prance with all their might,
Bouncing joy under sunlight.
Grass blades giggle as I stroll,
Nature's jesters, full of soul.

Harvesting Joy Beneath the Sun

Fruits are blushing on the vine,
While I'm sipping lemon-lime.
A basket full of silly dreams,
Laughter bursting at the seams.

Breezes toss the hats we wear,
Twirl and dance without a care.
Every giggle, every cheer,
Harvest happiness right here.

Serenity Found in Verdant Corners

In shady spots, the squirrels play,
Chasing shadows all the day.
Leafy hats on their small heads,
Planning mischief in their beds.

A nap beneath the shady tree,
Nature's comedy, wait and see.
With every rustle, every sigh,
Whimsical whispers drift on by.

Instants of Life in Light's Embrace

In the morning glow, I trip on a shoe,
The sun laughs out loud, bright as a stew.
Birds chirp in chorus, a confetti of sound,
While I juggle my breakfast, hope it's not browned.

Cats chase their shadows, all wild and spry,
I sip my cold coffee, oh, how time flies by!
A squirrel in a hoodie steals my lunch out of sight,
I swear, he just winked, adding to my plight.

Sunlit Promise Among the Greens

Mismatched socks flutter in a breeze so sweet,
I dance with a dandelion, light on my feet.
The grass tickles toes, a prank played so sly,
While bees buzz in circles, making me sigh.

A frog in a bow tie croaks out a tune,
As I flip my pancake, it lands on the moon.
Mushrooms are giggling, all tucked in their beds,
Nature's shine keeps swirling inside all our heads.

Nature's Lullaby in Brightness

A flower snickers as it tickles my nose,
While a butterfly catches its own little pose.
Smiling trees share secrets in sunlight's warm grasp,
I reach out to hug one; it just makes me gasp.

Crickets wear sunglasses, strumming their strings,
A squirrel thinks it's cool, as everyone swings.
The light wraps around us like dreams in a quilt,
Each chuckle and giggle, a moment well-spilt.

Flourishing Under Celestial Hues

In the garden of whimsy, I lose track of time,
As tomatoes come waving, oh, how they prime!
Chasing my hat, the wind plays a game,
While flowers burst out, calling my name.

The sun paints the petals in laughter and cheer,
And I trip on a weed that grew far too near.
Daisies unite, their heads in the sky,
As life's little moments, they happily sigh.

Whispering Leaves in Warmth

In the garden, green whispers play,
Each leaf giggles in a breezy sway.
Petals tickle as they softly bounce,
Nature's giggles, oh how they pounce!

Sunbeams dance on the dewy ground,
Nature's laughter is all around.
A gentle breeze brings in a jest,
Bringing joy, it truly knows best!

Reviving Nature's Embrace

Branches wave like a friendly hand,
Warming shadows in this vibrant land.
Chirping birds join in with a song,
Nature knows how to keep spirits strong!

Fluffy clouds drift with a grin,
Playing peek-a-boo, they won't let you in.
Flowers bow with a floral twist,
In this laughter, none can resist!

Luminous Serenity in Bloom

Jokes are hidden in the garden's hues,
A bloom of laughter, with teasing views.
Funny faces in the petals' spread,
A comical bloom, where giggles tread!

Daisies whisper silly little jokes,
While sunflowers swish like jovial blokes.
In every bud, a chuckle's found,
Nature's comedy, joyfully unbound!

Heartbeats of the Sun-kissed

Tickling rays, bright like a grin,
With each heartbeat, giggles begin.
Sun-kissed cheeks of daffodils bloom,
Laughter echoes in brightening rooms!

Breezes chuckle while the bees hum,
In this vibrant place, oh how fun!
Nature's cheer, a vibrant spree,
Where every moment is full of glee!

Sunlit Sanctum

In the corner, it sits quite green,
Winking softly, a leafy queen.
Basking in rays, the sun's warm kiss,
Whispers of fun, can't be amiss.

With each little poke, it sways with glee,
Sharing jokes, just with me.
Mirthful vibes in a sunny nook,
A plant with dreams, yeah, take a look!

Radiant Leaves

Oh my leaves, so bright and bold,
Smiles from you, a sight to behold.
If you could talk, you'd crack a joke,
Sipping sunbeam's laughter, no need to poke.

Twirling in light, they dance with flair,
Catching giggles, floating in air.
No other flora can match your cheer,
Every glance at you brings smiles near!

Warm Heart

With warmth so bright, it steals the show,
Radiating joy, like a flow.
A cuddle in green, a giggle surprise,
Life's comedy written in its wise eyes.

Tickles the sun with every sway,
Never dull, brightens the day.
A heart that's green, and full of mirth,
What a wonder, this leafy birth!

Embracing the Glow

Nestled here in a sunny spot,
Funny stories, it's got a lot.
A joke about sunbeams, quite absurd,
Leaves laughing loudly, haven't you heard?

Casting shadows, spreads the joy,
Prancing about, like a playful toy.
Sun-soaked moments weaves a yarn,
In the glow of cheer, it's never worn!

Verdant Dreams of Radiance

In dreams of green, where laughter flows,
A chatter of leaves, oh how it glows!
Each beam a punchline, each petal a grin,
Life's little secrets held deep within.

Marveling at how you sprout with flair,
Wit wrapped in green, beyond compare.
With every nod and a bright-eyed grin,
Sunshine's partner, it's here to win!

Caress of the Earth's Embrace

In a garden where giggles bloom,
Plants talk gossip, causing a zoom.
Petunias blush, gossiping near,
Lettuce links arms, spreading good cheer.

Worms dance underground, what a sight!
Dirt becomes warm with pure delight.
The sunlight tickles; soon it's a race,
Nature's laughter claims every space.

A snail in a tie takes a slow stroll,
While bees debate who's the best goal.
Butterflies flaunt in their fancy attire,
Each day's antics never seem to tire.

So join the fiesta, come take a look,
Life's quirky pages—just like a book.
In this patch of whimsy, joy is unfurled,
Earth's embrace tickles the whole wide world.

Warmth Beneath Verdant Canopy

Underneath leaves, a secret fair,
Squirrels chuckle, do you dare?
Chipmunks wager on acorn flair,
Sunbeams dance through the fragrant air.

Mushrooms mutter in hats of cheer,
While slugs debate who's the best near.
With sun's caress on the tender soil,
Life's silly antics are bound to uncoil.

A robin croons in a wobbly tone,
While ants march in a line, not alone.
Overhead, clouds toss shadows about,
Nature's shenanigans, never a doubt.

When dusk arrives, the laughter grows,
Fireflies join in, a light show bestows.
Under the green, life swings and sways,
In our leafy haven, joy always plays.

Sunkissed Sanctuary

In the heart of this sunny retreat,
Lizards sunbathe in tiny, warm seats.
Daisies giggle as they poke their heads,
While a frog brings news from the riverbeds.

The sun spreads joy like butter on toast,
With bees buzzing in a bustling ghost.
A breeze whispers secrets, oh what fun,
As nature leads dances under the sun.

Gummy worms wriggle, the dirt's soft bed,
For ants, the buffet is never misread.
The thrill of nature, so vivid and bright,
A whimsical world, a pure delight.

So let's celebrate every fanfare,
For in nature's arms, not a soul can despair.
In our sunkissed sanctuary, life's art,
Where laughter and sunshine sprinkle the heart.

Nature's Nurturing Glow

In the meadow, shenanigans thrive,
Caterpillars waltz, feel so alive.
Dandelions throw a wild feast,
While the moon takes peek, no kidding—at least.

A raccoon performs a moonlit show,
Juggling acorns, then stealing the glow.
Crickets chatter in a merry old choir,
While the starlight blankets, lifting up higher.

Rose bushes gossip about a new bloom,
Tulips giggle, dancing round the room.
As shadows leap and flicker about,
Nature's mischief, cannot live without.

So step into this laughter-filled abode,
Where every nook has its own little code.
With the earth's soft embrace—a delightful flow,
In the heart of the woods, we nurture the grow.

Bright Horizons of Verdant Hopes

In pots of green, dreams do dance,
With leaves that twirl in sunlit chance.
Each sprout a giggle, each bloom a cheer,
They tease the clouds to stay quite near.

The sunlight winks, a playful tease,
As plants jump up like they're on knees.
With every petal, there's a grin,
Nature's laughter, where fun begins.

Dancing shadows on the wall,
Swaying gently, having a ball.
A garden party, no need for shoes,
In this wild world, we just can't lose.

With colors bright, the smiles spread,
In botanical realms, our worries shed.
A garden joke, we all can share,
Sprouting happiness, beyond compare.

Sheltered by Sunshine's Tenderness

Underneath a leafy cover,
Giggling flowers, oh what a lover!
Sunbeams tickle each vibrant leaf,
In this warm glow, we find belief.

Critters scamper in playful spree,
With butterflies joining, oh what glee!
The air is thick with silly schemes,
As sunshine drips like honeyed dreams.

Potted pals start to unite,
A shameless dance in the golden light.
Whispering secrets, roots entwined,
In this cozy world, joy is defined.

Laughter echoes in the lush green,
In nature's warmth, we've all been seen.
So raise a toast to leafy friends,
In sunlit shades, the fun never ends.

Revitalizing Dreams in Flora

In the garden where giggles grow,
Plants are gossiping, don't you know?
With vibrant hues, they boast and brag,
While bees buzz along in a friendly drag.

Roots are twirling, seeking light,
Each leaf a smile, oh what a sight!
Dandelions don their crowns with pride,
In this botanical ball, dreams collide.

Sprouts on a mission, just can't sit still,
As they reach for the sun, there's a thrill.
Here, laughter blooms like wildflowers,
Each petal bursting, sweet with powers.

Nature's comedy, bright and free,
Where every plant can sing and be.
In verdant dreams, we can't resist,
Join the fun, it's a sunny twist!

Whispers of Life Glorified by Rays

Under sunbeams, mischief brews,
In the garden, plants play their dues.
They whisper jokes in leafy tones,
While sunbeams tickle their tiny bones.

Each bloom a punchline, ready to throw,
As butterflies flutter, putting on a show.
The daisies giggle, can you guess why?
Because the sun is the ultimate spy.

In every corner, a joke is sown,
Petals are laughter, clearly shown.
With bees as comedians, buzzing bright,
This flora fest is pure delight.

So let's embrace the sunny cheer,
And join the plants in laughter here.
For every leaf has tales to share,
In this garden realm, fun is everywhere.

Vibrance Found in Quiet Places

In a pot where silence hums,
Green limbs dance, nothing comes.
Whispers tickle leaves so bright,
A hidden party, pure delight.

Among the calm, a laughter bursts,
Where thirsty roots quench their thirsts.
When shadows play, the light's a tease,
It's nature's gift, just take it, please!

Glimmers of Joy Among the Greens

A sprout peeks out with a cheeky grin,
Stretching tall, saying, 'Let the fun begin!'
With every drop of rain that falls,
It wiggles, giggles, and breaks down walls.

In fields of green, a joke takes flight,
With sunbeams shining, oh what a sight!
Nature's jester, so sprightly and free,
Creating smiles, just wait and see!

Nourished by the Sun's Embrace

In the morning, warmth doth kiss,
A leafy friend, who cannot miss.
It drinks up rays, a sunny feast,
A joker's charm, never the least.

Beneath the rays, a secret lies,
With every twist, a sneak surprise!
Roots wiggle with a happy tune,
The garden laughs, beneath the moon.

Nature's Canvas of Light and Growth

On canvas green, colors collide,
A painter's brush, where glee will bide.
Petals twirl like dancers bright,
In this gallery, pure delight.

With chortles brewing on the breeze,
Leaves shimmy, swirling with such ease.
In every nook, a giggle's found,
Nature's humor knows no bound!

Whispering Leaves Under Sunlight

In the garden, trees do sway,
Whisper secrets, come what may.
Leaves that dance, with laughter loud,
Shout to the sun, they're feeling proud.

Bugs in suits, and ants in line,
Hosting tea, in the sun's warm shine.
Twirling petals, what a sight,
Nature's circus, pure delight.

Tickled ferns, with giggles bright,
Bouncing curls in the warm daylight.
Oh, the grass, it joins the cheer,
While blooms chase away the drear.

So come and join this leafy glee,
In this show, wild and free.
For laughter echoes in the breeze,
Under sunlight, among the trees.

Garden of Solace

In this patch of bloomin' fun,
Flowers wear their brightest pun.
Petals wearing silly hats,
Chasing down the bouncy mats.

Worms in ties, on their way to work,
Dancing slowly, what a perk!
Caterpillars making bets,
Who'll be first to grow their jets?

Sunshine smiles upon the blooms,
While bees hum jazzy tunes.
Even shadows join the spree,
In a garden, wild and free.

With every rustle of the grass,
Nature's giggles travel fast.
Join the laughter, come and play,
In this joyous, bright bouquet.

Illuminated by Green

Here comes the green, all aglow,
Plants lined up in a fun row.
Frogs in shades, sipping their tea,
Making puns that tickle me.

Branches sport their leafy wear,
Waving at the sunlit air.
Lizards laughing, doing flips,
While birds join in with chirpy quips.

Lilies wink, they're in on it,
Tickled by the sun, they sit.
Daisies gossip, what a chat,
In this patch, where fun is at.

The sun peeks in, a playful sprite,
Lighting up the garden bright.
Every critter, every breeze,
Whispers joy, such sweet decrees.

Gentle Sunlit Haven

In a haven where the sunbeams play,
Silly bugs have come to stay.
Ladybugs chuckle on a leaf,
Even grasshoppers join in brief.

Bouncing blooms in colors cheer,
Flutter by with no trace of fear.
Sunscreen on, the daisies pose,
While butterflies flaunt their fancy clothes.

The toads croak rhythms of delight,
Teaching frogs to dance just right.
Bumblebees buzz with all their might,
Creating symphonies in flight.

So let's sip on sunshine's light,
Join this garden, take a bite.
In this haven, joy does thrive,
Where every heart feels so alive.

Dawn's Gentle Caress on Flora

In the morning's soft embrace,
Petals yawn and stretch their face.
Roses whisper silly jokes,
While daisies tease the morning folks.

Bees don tiny hats with pride,
A ladybug joins the joyful ride.
Flowers giggle in the breeze,
Dancing lightly, oh so at ease.

Sunlight sprinkles golden gleams,
As stems twist, the grass all beams.
Silly shadows play around,
A floral circus in the ground.

Laughter bubbles, warmth in tow,
Each bloom sporting a funny bow.
With nature's charm and hoot so grand,
The garden's laughter fills the land.

Vibrant Life Beneath a Bright Sky

Underneath a canvas blue,
Squirrels chatter, they're a crew.
Flowers flaunt their vibrant hues,
Dancing in their joyful blues.

Frogs with ties croak out a tune,
While butterflies play hide and swoon.
Clouds drift by, a silly bunch,
In a game of lunchtime lunch.

Grasshoppers hop with leaps so grand,
In a race, they lose their stand.
Caterpillars' parties drag,
Velvet salads, leafy swag!

Buzzing jokes from bees on high,
Make the daisies laugh and sigh.
In vibrant life, the fun won't die,
As nature's doodles dance and fly.

Sun-drenched Dreams of Healing

A soft glow falls on sleepy heads,
Where dandelions dance in threads.
Sunbeams tickle, oh so bright,
With dreams of laughter, pure delight.

Cacti wear sunglasses upside-down,
Their prickly faces flip and frown.
While sunflowers spin around the sun,
Yelling, "We're not done, just begun!"

Zooming ants in tiny cars,
Racing by beneath the stars.
Lemonade rivers flow so sweet,
While nature's disco feels the beat.

Healing hearts in the warm embrace,
With giggles echoing through this space.
The sun sets low, the stars now gleam,
In nature's clinic, we all dream.

Brushstrokes of Nature's Glow

With every stroke, the sun does play,
A quirky palette, bright and gay.
The trees don socks of green and gold,
While daisies giggle, pure and bold.

The breeze is teasing, pulling leaves,
As if it knows just how to tease.
Painted skies in orange hues,
Nature's canvas, bright with news!

Fungi wear their hats so tall,
While seedlings gather for a ball.
Silly critters paint the town,
With nature's sparkle, never frown.

As colors swirl in laughter's clutch,
Even rocks can feel the touch.
With brushstrokes wild, and hearts aglow,
Nature's jesters steal the show.

Tides of Green and Gold

In a garden bright, the plants do sway,
Chasing squirrels that hop and play.
With leaves of green, they gossip loud,
Chatting secrets in a leafy crowd.

The sun peeks in with a cheeky grin,
A dance of shadows begins to spin.
Tulips giggle, a colorful jest,
While daisies bloom, feeling quite blessed.

Mischief blooms in every petal,
Laughter rides on the breeze, so gentle.
The bees buzz by, a clumsy flight,
A comedy show in the morning light.

So here we are, amid colors bold,
In nature's arms, a joy to behold.
Life's little quirks, painted so bright,
A tapestry woven in pure delight.

Sun's Dance with the Leaf

The sun tiptoes on leaves of jade,
Performing tricks in the afternoon shade.
A leaf, quite slick, does a little glide,
As laughter echoes, joy can't hide.

With every flicker, a giggle escapes,
The flowers are blushes, just like red grapes.
Petunias chuckle at butterflies' flits,
While orchids debate the best of wits.

A gentle breeze carries off a joke,
Tickling blooms until they poke.
The daisies dance with wild abandon,
Creating mischief, oh, aren't they handsome!

But soon the sun takes a bow and departs,
Leaving soft whispers in nature's hearts.
With memories bright of laughter alive,
In twilight's hush, the giggles survive.

Botanical Embrace of Daylight

Morning stretches with a sleepy yawn,
As dew drops shimmer on the lawn.
Plants engage in a morning chat,
Deciding who wears the silliest hat.

Every bud has a tale to tell,
With petals that laugh and laugh so well.
Sunlight spills like a river of gold,
And stories unfold in hues bold.

The ferns wave hello with a sassy sway,
While rabbits hop, ready to play.
Such whimsy fills the garden air,
A circus of flora, beyond compare.

In nature's arms, we find our glee,
With silly plants, the best company.
So let the laughter ring out high,
In the botanical embrace, we fly!

Nature's Warm Touch

Nature chuckles with a soothing breeze,
As sunlight tickles the sturdy trees.
Leaves whisper jokes, light as the air,
While the flowers twist, not a single care.

Butterflies flutter with comic flair,
Playing tag without a single scare.
The daisies roll with laughter so free,
Nature's warm touch is the place to be.

Grasshoppers leap like kids at play,
In a whimsical ballet, come what may.
Each bloom shares a laugh, it's quite the show,
As petals dance, our hearts overflow.

So let us bask in this wild delight,
Where nature's embrace is warm and bright.
In a world full of joys, both big and small,
Nature invites us to laugh with all.

Fields of Light and Leaf

In a garden so bright and alive,
Where wriggly worms dance, and bees always strive.
The plants wear their green, a jolly parade,
While sunlight giggles in a leafy charade.

The dandelions gossip, spreading delight,
As petals all shimmer in the warm, golden light.
While the tulips don sunhats with flair,
And the roses blush pink, with sweetness to spare.

Radiance Unfurled in Bloom.

When blossoms burst forth with a wink and a grin,
The daisies declare it's a riotous win!
With petals that twirl in a whimsical dance,
And bees that buzz by in a joyful romance.

Sprinklers cheer up each wandering toe,
While sunflowers tall steal the marvelous show.
Snapdragons snap, with a laugh in their voice,
In fields where all blossoms rejoice in their choice.

Radiant Echoes of Green

The grass tickles toes and sings with delight,
As the squirrels chase shadows, what a silly sight!
Butterflies flutter, all bright and so bold,
While the sun sips its coffee, not too hot or cold.

Lemonade stands pop up, full of sweet cheer,
As the daisies decide to play hide-and-seek here.
The laughter of petals fills up the wide air,
Grasshoppers hop in a comedic affair.

Embrace of the Sunlight

Oh, the sun is a joker, with rays that tease,
Bringing warmth to our toes and whispering 'please'.
Frogs in their shades, with sunglasses on tight,
Croak out their laughter from morning till night.

Giggling flowers hold hands in delight,
While clouds float above, it's a marvelous sight.
The breeze joins the fun, swaying all around,
In the embrace of the sunlight, joy can be found.

Sun's Radiance on Green Dreams

Bright beams dance on leaves so wide,
Nature's laughter, fun can't hide.
Green soldiers stretch up to the sky,
Making sunlight giggle as it passes by.

A plant parade in sunny clothes,
Each frond winks, and sunlight glows.
Chasing shadows, they do flip,
Nature's comedy, a joyful trip.

In the garden, jokes abound,
Tiny critters prance around.
The sun's warm kiss, oh what a show,
Green dreams sparkle in golden glow.

Underneath the azure dome,
Laughter lends the plants a home.
With every beam, their spirits rise,
In leafy lanes, the fun never dies.

Chasing Light Through Leafy Lanes

A leaf that giggles, oh so spry,
Winks at clouds that hurry by.
Chasing rays like kids at play,
Turns the garden into a ballet.

Branches sway, a dance of cheer,
Whispers of joy, can you hear?
Sunbeams tickle every stem,
Nature's jesters, a leafy gem.

The grass tickles your toes anew,
As sunshine giggles, laughter brew.
Petals rustle with cheeky cheer,
Chasing the light, we hold it dear.

In leafy lanes where pranks unfold,
Green dreams chase the sun, they're bold.
What a show, what a delight,
Nature's jesters bask in light!

Resilient Hearts in Nature's Glow

Little sprouts with hearts aglow,
Stand up tall, put on a show.
With roots so strong, they laugh at fate,
In nature's realm, they congregate.

Sunshine chuckles as they sway,
Braving storms that come their way.
With friendly nudges from the breeze,
They tease the clouds with leafy tease.

In the dirt, they play and dig,
Life's a dance, a lively jig.
Through the struggles, they stand proud,
Little warriors, joy unbowed.

In every shadow, there's a grin,
Resilient hearts, they wear their skin.
With sunlight's laughter, they ignite,
A funny fight; it feels so right.

Glowing Wonders of the Earth

Beneath the sun, the world sings bright,
With laughter echoing, pure delight.
Every leaf, a tiny muse,
Swaying softly, they refuse to lose.

Nature's tricks, a merry spree,
Dancing light, it's plain to see.
Colors burst, a cheerful plot,
Who knew the soil had such a lot?

Tiny flowers share a laugh,
Tickled by the sun's warm path.
In glorious hues, they strut their stuff,
Reminding us that joy is enough.

With each sunrise, a brand new prank,
Nature's joy, a bubbly tank.
In glowing wonders, giggles spark,
Filling hearts till it's pitch dark.

Bright Expressions of Leafy Love

In the garden, plants all grinned,
Their laughter sprouted with the wind.
A cactus tried to join the fun,
But poked himself—oh, such a pun!

The daisies danced in skirts of white,
While sunflowers bowed to the morning light.
What's a flower? Just petals and glee,
Buddies in bloom, as happy as can be.

The ivy giggled, hugging a wall,
As critters chuckled, giving a call.
A shrub wore glasses, thinking it wise,
Reading stories of sunshine in the skies.

With nature's humor, life does start,
In this leafy realm, we live, we part.
So plant a joke, watch laughter grow,
And let your joys like petals flow!

Nature's Gracious Gift of Light

With morning dew, the leaves unite,
Each droplet shining, oh so bright.
A snail slid by, too slow for hype,
His pace was set—no rush, no type.

The sun peeked through with a wink and cheer,
Saying, "Let's spread some warmth, my dear!"
The clouds looked fluffy, like whipped cream,
In this nature pot, life's a dream!

Rabbits playing hopscotch in the grass,
While kites and butterflies cheerfully pass.
The breeze whispered secrets, soft and light,
"Dance with me, my friend, take flight!"

Nature's giggles are ever so bold,
Each vine and twig has stories untold.
In this symphony of shades and gleam,
Let laughter echo—join the playful team!

When Green Meets the Golden Glow

Oh, the grass was verdant, lush, and fine,
As bees basked sweetly, sipping their wine.
A lawn chair joked, "I'm always on call!"
"Just sit back, relax!" it would bellow and sprawl.

The sunset blushed with a golden grin,
While critters gathered for a cheeky din.
Squirrels exchanged tales of nuts and cheese,
In a world where laughter flowed with ease.

As the moon arrived, the stars took flight,
The night wrapped itself in cozy delight.
"Why did the tree laugh?" asked a fern,
"Because it found a worm in its turn!"

Life's colors mingled in merry array,
In this garden party, who needs to sway?
Just spread your arms and embrace the glow,
When the green meets gold, let joy overflow!

Secrets Held in Nature's Embrace

In nature's arms, the whispers play,
A leaf told secrets in a cheeky way.
The rocks rolled their eyes at the gossipy breeze,
"Just chill out, buddy, and take it with ease!"

A toad croaked tunes, an opera at night,
Drawing laughs from the stars, oh what a sight!
The moon winked down with a silvery cheer,
"Let's keep this party going—I'm always near!"

Petunias pranced with rhythm so bold,
While tulips painted tales of the old.
Trees swayed and bent to the music's flow,
A canopy dance, all topped with a glow.

So here in this haven, we find our place,
Where every leaf holds a smile, a trace.
Embrace the laughter, let your heart race,
In nature's warm hug, we find our grace!

Vivid Hues of Comfort

In pots so bright, they laugh and sway,
Spiky and green, what a display!
They soak up light, no need for shade,
In this wild jungle, nature's parade.

With little hands, we give them care,
Whisper our secrets; they won't share.
Water them slow, don't make a splash,
They're the laughter, we're the bash!

Sipping some tea, they bask in cheer,
Coy little smiles, come gather near.
With humor growing, they bloom so bright,
Each prickly joke is pure delight.

Caught in a dance, they wiggle and twist,
A comedic touch that can't be missed.
Like friendly gnomes, they take the stage,
Offering giggles, they engage!

Sunlit Gardens of Resilience

In gardens where the laughter roams,
Our green companions find their homes.
Sun-kissed faces, bright and bold,
They share old jokes that never get old.

The sun peeks in, a golden grin,
Making sure the fun begins.
With every drop of gleaming light,
They send us chuckles, pure delight!

Each morning brings a playful tease,
As they stretch up high, like they're on ease.
With every breeze, they sway and dance,
Inviting us for a sunny chance.

From vibrant greens to shining gold,
Their joyous antics never get old.
In this merry patch, we all unite,
Managing smiles from day to night!

Touch of Light on Tender Leaves

Whispers of joy in every vein,
Silly stories, like gentle rain.
Each little leaf with a funny tale,
Dancing to rhythms in the gale.

With sunlight's poke, they giggle and sway,
Ticklish breeze, come join the play!
Green thumbs up for every cheer,
In their presence, worries disappear.

Every touch tells a lively jest,
They hold their ground, they know what's best.
Wrap us in warmth, a soft embrace,
In the garden, we find our place.

Tiny dramas in every sprout,
With playful plots we can't live without.
With all this fun under the sun,
Who needs a crown when we can run?

Gleaming Spirits of Summer

Spirits of summer, so bright and spry,
With twinkling eyes, they touch the sky.
Chasing shadows, they won't sit still,
Their laughter echoes, a joyous thrill.

Crisp in the breeze, they tease the light,
Frolicking freely, such a sight!
Each little sprout, a prank in store,
With antics that leave us wanting more.

As skies grow bright, their smiles do bloom,
Their quirky dance fills up the room.
Together we sway, like winds of cheer,
These lively greens, we hold so dear.

Beneath our care, they laugh and play,
Chasing away the dull and gray.
In the garden's heart, their joy will stay,
With gleaming spirits lighting the way!

Flourishing Spirits in Nature's Light

In the garden, plants do dance,
With shiny leaves, they take a chance.
Whispers of joy through branches flow,
Even the weeds put on a show!

Sunbeams tickle all around,
While critters hop from ground to ground.
Petals giggle in the breeze,
Chasing shadows like happy bees!

Laughter sprinkles from the flowers,
It feels like playtime for the hours.
Nature's glee is here to stay,
As we bask in this glorious play!

Green thumbs up, the fun's not done,
Every sprout smiles under the sun.
With cheerful hues and a sprinkle of shade,
Life's a garden, let's not trade!

Beats of Joy in Flora's Embrace

In the meadow, petals sway,
Each bloom sings a bright ballet.
Grassy beats thump beneath our feet,
Nature's rhythm can't be beat!

Buzzing bees join in the cheer,
A fuzzy band that draws us near.
With pollen dance-offs all around,
Even the daisies twirl unwound!

Fragrant scents make noses twitch,
Who knew herbs could be so rich?
Plants giggle, sharing their flair,
In this orchestra beyond compare!

A sunflower winks as we prance,
In sunshine's glow, we take our chance.
With bloomin' vibes and carefree shows,
Life's a garden where fun grows!

Daybreak Colors Alive with Hope

With dawn's light, the colors gleam,
Nature wakes, and so must we dream.
Bright oranges and yellows break,
It's like a breakfast for the brave!

Dewdrops glisten as they play,
Each moment adds a splash of ray.
Petals yawn in fresh delight,
Morning giggles take to flight!

Butterflies don their fancy suits,
As grasshoppers tune their flutes.
With every chirp and rustling sound,
Hope wraps us in its joyful bound!

In this canvas, shades collide,
Every hue lets laughter slide.
Let's kickstart joy, like the dawn's spark,
Life's a circus — come join the park!

Lush Tones of Bliss and Growth

In verdant seas, the laughter flows,
Where even cacti wear their bows.
Ferns wave like they own the space,
In this wild and silly place!

Whirling leaves in playful flight,
Tickle our toes, oh what a sight!
Roots play hide and seek down low,
While flowers jive in grand tableau!

With colors bright, we shout hooray,
Each sprout fashioning its own display.
In this green world of fun and cheer,
Lush tones remind us to persevere!

Nature's giggles ignite the day,
As joyful hues lead us astray.
Let's twirl through gardens, hearts aglow,
In laughter's wake, let's freely grow!

Sun-kissed Souls in Harmony

In the glow of a blazing ball,
We dance like fools, having a ball.
With shades too big and laughter loud,
We're the silliest crew in this sunlit crowd.

Butterflies want to steal our style,
But we just grin and stay a while.
With hair that frizzes and spirits high,
We throw our hands up, reaching the sky.

The sun might scorch, but we don't care,
We apply more lotion, a dazzling affair.
Fried hair do's and hot dog charms,
We're here to soak up all the warm arms.

Bikinis bright and flip-flops loose,
Together we laugh, oh what a hoot!
Golden rays, come out and play,
Life feels endless, hip-hip-hooray!

Flourishing in the Brightness of Day

Radiant rays make shadows dance,
With ice cream cones, we take our chance.
Sun hats large and all the flair,
We strut along without a care.

Sizzling sidewalks, giggles bloom,
As ants parade with quite the zoom.
We sip our drinks in fancy jars,
And dodge wild kids chasing stars.

Sunburned noses and silly squints,
We conquer parks, no need for hints.
With mismatched socks and summer cheer,
Each moment sparkles, bright and clear.

As daylight wraps us in its glow,
We play like kids, just letting go.
Under blue skies, life feels so grand,
Let's kick up dirt and make our stand!

Gentle Dews on Vital Green

Morning breaks with laughter sweet,
Dewdrops glisten, oh what a treat!
Each leaf a stage, our antics unfold,
In the green embrace, life's shimmering gold.

Flowers giggle with petals wide,
As we stomp through the bushes, side by side.
With playful pranks, we roll in the grass,
Singing tunes that let worries pass.

Nature's cloak, a vibrant scene,
We chase the wind, feeling so keen.
Jogging in circles, what a sight,
Our joy spills over, pure delight.

The world our playground, we leap and bound,
In dewy meadows where laughter's found.
With smiles and shenanigans all around,
On this vital green, joy is profound!

Warmth in the Face of Life

Life's a joke with the sun as the punch,
We laugh it off, never losing our lunch.
With radiant beams shining bright,
We embrace each challenge, full of light.

Tickled by warmth, we prance and play,
At the whim of the breeze, come what may.
Juggling lemons and melting ice,
We chase the fun; it's oh-so-nice!

Welcomes abound, as we trip and fall,
On splashy puddles, down we sprawl.
Our spirits rise like the sun at noon,
A glorious dance, a silly tune.

So let the warmth each moment bless,
As we turn life's fuss into jest.
Together we shine, so bright, so bold,
In the warmth of laughter, our hearts unfold!

A Haven of Green Light

In a jungle of pots, so green and bright,
A plant had a party, what a funny sight!
With leaves waving wildly, it danced all day,
Sipping sunshine tea, in a hipster way.

A cactus crashed in, looking quite spiked,
Claiming he brought the most exciting hike!
But the leafy ones laughed, they knew the deal,
While sunbathing, they made quite the meal.

Clouds drifted in, causing a fuss,
Yet the jokes kept them rolling, they laughed with us.
"Don't rain on my parade," the tall fern quipped,
As the blooms burst into giggles, slightly flipped.

In their haven of green, under sun's warm light,
They knew every day would be pure delight.
So they danced and they sang, in their leafy spree,
Creating a ruckus, wild and free!

Soothing Sunlit Embrace

A sunbeam tickled, a laughter shared,
With leaves all a-jiggle, they really didn't care.
"Too much light?" one sunflower teased,
But the geranium just hummed, completely pleased.

"Let's stretch our petals, let's reach for the sun!
We'll dance till the moon says our time's done!"
The daisies cheered loudly, with a twist and twirl,
As the garden burst forth, in a lively whirl.

A bumblebee buzzed, trying to join in,
But tripped on a flower, oh, what a sin!
"Watch where you're buzzing, you clumsy old bee!"
The pansies all snickered, under the tree.

Yet in this bright patch, all worries took flight,
With sunshine and laughter, the day felt just right.
So they basked in the glow, full of fun and grace,
In the sun's warm embrace, finding joy in each place.

The Gentle Glow of Nature

In the warmth of the day, they gathered around,
With whispers of laughter and soft nature's sound.
"Oh look at that bloom," said the cheeky old rose,
"Who wears such a crown? It's quite the fine nose!"

With critters all hopping, they joined in the jest,
There's humor in petals, like nature's own fest.
The daisies played tag, the violets would tease,
While the sun made everyone feel as they please.

"Last one to bloom has to do a jig!"
Cried a witty old fern, feeling rather big.
And so they all danced, in a comical whirl,
With twirls and with giggles, each leaf gave a twirl.

Their roots grounded deep, but their spirits flew high,
In a green universe, where time passed them by.
With the gentle glow shining, nothing felt wrong,
And the laughter of nature sang them a song.

Earth's Embrace in the Sun

In a grassy old field, where the daisies sprout,
The critters convened for a picnic, no doubt.
They chewed on the sun, danced 'neath the skies,
While butterflies giggled, with colorful ties.

"Who's the funniest plant?" asked a curious bee,
"I bet it's the dandelion, wild and free!"
But the clover just blushed, with a mischievous grin,
As the whole meadow chuckled, letting the fun begin.

With roots intertwined, they created a show,
Where vines told the tales of all they know.
"It's not just for shade, it's a place to unwind,
With laughter as fresh as the great outdoors find!"

Under soft sunlight, the laughter rang true,
In a world full of wonders, colorful and new.
So they basked in the joy, in their radiant sun,
For nature's embrace is the best kind of fun!

The Dance of Light and Serenity

In the garden, bright and bold,
Dancing leaves in stories told.
Sunbeams waltz with joyful flair,
While shadows giggle, unaware.

Buzzy bees tap dance on blooms,
Sipping sweetness, chasing glooms.
Plants prance lightly in the breeze,
While flowers tease the bumblebees.

A lizard sings a silly tune,
Basking under the afternoon.
Nature's revelry takes its flight,
As critters join the playful light.

So laugh a little, join the fest,
In this green haven, we are guests.
With joy we sway, with heartbeats kind,
In the dance of light, we unwind.

Heartfelt Whispers Among the Botany

Whispers float through leafy greens,
Chatty crickets share their scenes.
The blush of petals soft and bright,
Hold secrets whispered by daylight.

A sunflower with a cheeky grin,
Winks at passers, let games begin!
With cheeky turns and silly hops,
The willow eavesdrops on the flops.

Under skies so wonderfully blue,
A worm in boots declares what's true.
"Life is funny, don't you see?
Just laugh a lot, and we'll be free!"

So join the tales, and share a smile,
In the garden, stay awhile.
For among the greens and sunny cheer,
Laughter blooms, and joy is near.

Sunlit Revelations Amidst the Green

A sprout with shades of emerald dreams,
Spills the tea on sunshine beams.
She spills her love, a radiant glow,
To tickle toes and warm the grow.

While cacti boast of prickly style,
With jokes that leave you in a pile.
"Here's my point," they quip with glee,
"Just don't sit close; it's not for free!"

The daisies chuckle in the breeze,
Twirling tales with each gentle tease.
"Life's a garden, come take a stroll,
With laughter's seeds, we thrive and rol."

Under the sun, the hours fly,
With chortles shared, we reach the sky.
So dance with glee and let hearts sing,
In nature's laughter, joy takes wing.

Nurtured by the Gentle Rays

Giggling grass stretches for the light,
Whispering secrets while taking flight.
With every sunbeam, a cheeky tease,
Nature's embrace puts minds at ease.

A butterfly flutters, bold and free,
Fashion opinions, carefree decree.
"Join the fun, dance like a flower,
Let's bloom together in this hour!"

A lazy frog croaks out a pun,
While basking in the warmth of sun.
"Come join the pond, don't be so shy,
Hop on in, let's splash, oh my!"

So gather round, and share a laugh,
In nature's playground, we carve a path.
With gentle rays our hearts embrace,
In botanical joy, we find our place.

Healing Touch of the Petals

In a pot with a frown, a plant does sit,
Waiting for sunlight, oh, where is it?
With a sprinkle of water, it gives a grin,
Saying, "Don't worry, let the fun begin!"

Reaching for snacks, it sways with delight,
Dancing to tunes that feel just right.
Who knew a plant could be such a tease?
Making me laugh while it sways in the breeze!

Serenity in the Sun's Warm Grasp

Golden beams touch a cozy leaf,
Spreading smiles, relieving grief.
"Hey there, sunshine, pour on the rays!"
The plant giggles, in its own quirky ways.

Catching some shade, it takes a break,
Whispers, "This heat? Just a piece of cake!"
With a poky leaf, it playfully jabs,
Claiming the sun, like a cozy fab.

Leaves of Hope Under Blue Skies

Underneath a sky that's bright and clear,
Dances a plant, spreading cheer.
"Look at me! I'm the king of green!"
In its leafy crown, pure bliss is seen.

With every droplet that falls nearby,
It sings a tune, oh so spry.
"A quick drink is all that I crave,
And then off to show how plants can wave!"

Gentle Hearth of Verdant Bliss

Gather around, my leafy friends,
As the sun descends, and laughter blends.
In the warmth, we swap silly tales,
Of windy days and thunderous gales.

With a stretch and a yawn, the leaves come alive,
In this cozy hearth, we thrive and jive.
"Watch me mimic your dance!" it cries,
A comedy show under starlit skies!

Embrace of Healing Light

In a pot, they sit so proud,
Sunglasses on, they laugh out loud.
With spiky hair that shines so bright,
Giving hugs in morning light.

They whisper secrets to the sun,
"Don't be shy, let's have some fun!"
Waving leaves like little hands,
Making merry with sunbaked sands.

When clouds come near, they make a stance,
Spreading joy with a little dance.
With drips of rain, they soak and spin,
Giggling at the storm within.

Their healing charm, a sprightly jest,
Bringing smiles, they are the best.
In every corner, bright and spry,
These little greens lift spirits high.

Tender Green Whispers

Little leaves with laughter grow,
In their world of sunlit glow.
Tickle roots with a gentle tease,
Bending softly in the breeze.

Joking 'bout the bugs that crawl,
"Hey, we're not a salad, after all!"
Cackling in their leafy dreams,
Plucking joy from sunny beams.

Each sprout has stories soaked in cheer,
Of how they dance from year to year.
"Chill, the sun is where it's at,
Catch the rays and look quite fat!"

So gather round, enjoy the sight,
Of tender greens in happy light.
Nature's laughter, let it flow,
In sunny patches, watch them grow.

Radiance in Soft Embrace

Cactus friends in cozy chairs,
Winking at the passing stares.
"We're not prickly, just a bit shy,
Let's chit-chat and watch clouds fly!"

In sunshine pools, they bask and beam,
Crafting joys like a sweet daydream.
"Hey, did you see that bug do flips?
A circus act from nature's scripts!"

With petals soft, they face the day,
Tickling cheeks in their green ballet.
Open arms for hugs they bring,
Radiance blooms with every swing.

So let's toast with lemonade,
To friends who love playful charades.
In their warmth, the laughter blends,
In that glow, the fun never ends.

Sun-Kissed Serenity

Leaves of laughter in a line,
Joyful greens that twist and twine.
"We've got the sun, let's bask away,
And tell the world it's playtime, yay!"

With shadows stretching on the ground,
They dance around, a silly sound.
"Join the party, don't delay,
Nature's here, come out to play!"

A gentle breeze brings giggles near,
Secret whispers, lend an ear.
"They think we're just plants but oh,
We're also the stars of the show!"

So grab a drink, sit back and see,
What joyful green friends bring to me.
In sunny patches, let's unite,
For laughter shared is pure delight.

Botanical Harmony

In a pot, a greenling smiles,
Sipping sunlight, stacking styles.
With a wink, it stretches tall,
Whispers secrets, won't let fall.

A friend with spines but heart of gold,
Tales of warmth in soil retold.
Waving leaves with sassy flair,
Joking in the garden fair.

When the breeze begins to play,
Wiggles roots, a dance display.
Who needs soap when nature's here?
Laughter blooms, the path is clear.

In this patch, we all belong,
A chorus of the green and strong.
So come and join this leafy spree,
Where giggles grow and plants run free.

Gentle Wakes of Warmth

Morning light, a cheerful tease,
Tugging petals, swaying trees.
Waking up a sleepy crew,
Nature's laugh, a sunny view.

Twirling leaves, oh, what a sight!
Plants in pajamas, just so bright.
A breeze struts through, a playful kick,
Tickling stems, oh what a trick!

Comfy roots, they stretch and yawn,
Giggling softly, all forlorn.
Buds and blooms, a cozy chat,
Who knew plants could play like that?

Sunshine's grin, a playful wink,
In this web, we dance and link.
With every leaf, a tale we weave,
A world where joy is what we believe.

Radiant Resilience

A little sprout, so boldly claims,
Its pot, a throne, in leafy games.
Against the odds, it stands so proud,
Waving cheer in nature's crowd.

With every gust, a little sway,
It giggles through the tough today.
Petals soft, but spiky too,
Who knew tough love could feel so new?

When raindrops fall, it makes a splash,
In muddy puddles, it's quite brash.
In storms and shine, it takes a bow,
Nature's drama, take a vow.

So here's to green, both bold and bright,
A plant with humor, sheer delight.
In the garden's riotous show,
Resilience blooms, as we all know.

Nature's Healing Touch

In a corner, something's twirling,
Tiny leaves, a dance unfurling.
With a chuckle, it makes me smile,
Nature's cure, worth every while.

Laughter lingers in the air,
Spiky hugs and scents so rare.
With each petal, a story's told,
Of sunny days and friendships bold.

Moonlit whispers, evening's tease,
Plant friends gather, aiming to please.
With cheeky grins, they watch me bloom,
Nature's spirits fill the room.

So here's to greens that spread such cheer,
Turning frowns into a happy sphere.
With fidgeting roots and sunny clutches,
Life's a giggle, nature's touches.

www.ingramcontent.com/pod-product-compliance
Lightning Source LLC
Chambersburg PA
CBHW070314120526
44590CB00017B/2667